# Contents

# Objects in the Sky

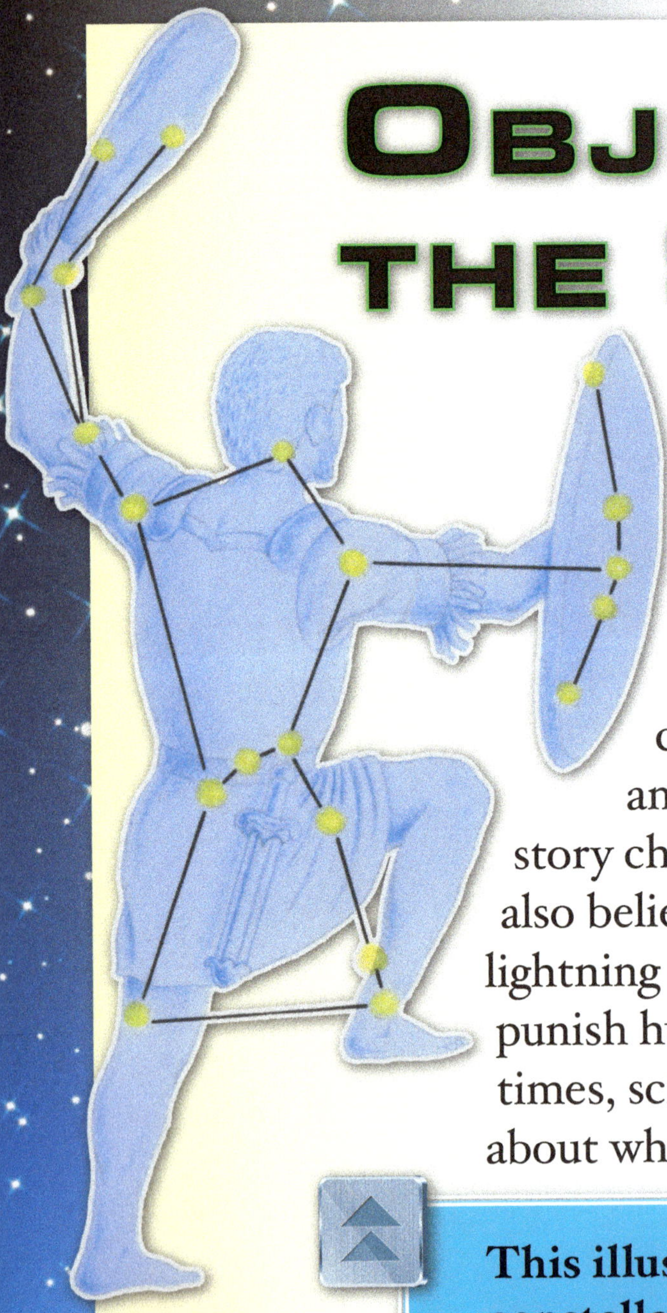

Since ancient times, people have tried to explain the things they could see in the sky. Different cultures have seen different patterns in the stars. They have named constellations after familiar animals, everyday objects, and story characters. Ancient peoples also believed that angry gods threw lightning bolts from the heavens to punish humans on Earth. Since these times, scientists have learned much about what is really in the sky.

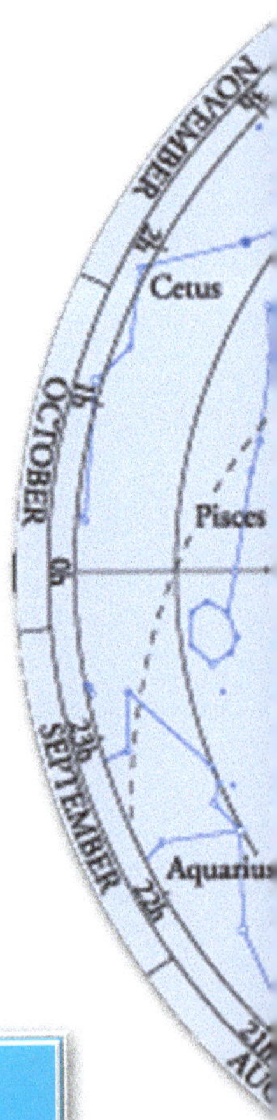


**This illustration shows the constellation Orion, named after the hunter in Greek mythology.**

LET'S FIND OUT! SPACE

# WHAT IS AN OBJECT IN THE SKY?

CHRISTINE POOLOS

Britannica Educational Publishing

IN ASSOCIATION WITH

ROSEN

EDUCATIONAL SERVICES

Published in 2015 by Britannica Educational Publishing (a trademark of Encyclopædia Britannica, Inc.) in association with The Rosen Publishing Group, Inc.
29 East 21st Street, New York, NY 10010



Distributed exclusively by Rosen Publishing.

To see additional Britannica Educational Publishing titles, go to rosenpublishing.com.

First Edition

**Britannica Educational Publishing**
J. E. Luebering: Director, Core Reference Group
Mary Rose McCudden: Editor, Britannica Student Encyclopedia

**Rosen Publishing**
Hope Lourie Killcoyne: Executive Editor
John Murphy: Editor
Nelson Sá: Art Director
Brian Garvey: Designer
Cindy Reiman: Photography Manager
Karen Huang: Photo Researcher

**Cataloging-in-Publication Data**

Poolos, Christine, author.
What is an object in the sky?/Christine Poolos.—First edition.
pages cm.—(Let's find out! Space)
Includes bibliographical references and index.
ISBN 978-1-62275-471-7 (library bound)—ISBN 978-1-62275-473-1 (pbk.)—ISBN 978-1-62275-474-8 (6-pack)
1. Astronomy—Juvenile literature. 2. Meteorology—Juvenile literature. I. Title.
QB46.P66 2015
520—dc23
2013048392

*Manufactured in the United States of America*

Photo Credits: Cover, p.1 (meteorite) Triff/Shutterstock.com; cover, p. 1 (background) argus/Shutterstock.com; p. 4 Dorling Kindersley/Vetta/Getty Images; pp. 4-5, 7, 10, 15, 18–19 (bottom), 22, 28 Encyclopædia Britannica, Inc.; pp. 6–7 Hubble Heritage Team/NASA; pp. 8–9 NASA, ESA, S. Beckwith (STScI), and The Hubble Heritage Team (STScI/AURA); p. 9 De Agostini/Getty Images; p. 11 © Stockbyte/Thinkstock; pp. 12–13 David Wall Photo/Lonely Planet Images/Getty Images; p. 13 Photo by Matt Payne of Colorado Springs, CO/Flickr/Getty Images; p. 14 NASA/JSC; pp. 16–17 MyLoupe/Universal Images Group/Getty Images; pp. 17, 18–19 (top), 20–21 (bottom) NASA; p. 21 (top) NASA Orbital Debris Program Office; pp. 22–23 L. Ferrarese (Johns Hopkins University) and NASA/ESA; pp. 24–25 (top) Flickr/Getty Images; pp. 24–25 (bottom) Michael S. Nolan/age fotostock/Getty Images; pp. 26–27 tropicalpix/E+/Getty Images; p. 27 GIPhotoStock/Photo Researchers/Getty Images; p. 29 Encyclopaedia Britannica/UIG//Getty Images; interior page borders © iStockphoto.com/twilightproductions.

## Constellations are among the many fascinating objects in the sky.

When people think of objects in the sky, they may think about planets, the Sun, the Moon, and the constellations. Many other bodies orbit Earth and the Sun, however. Some of these bodies are natural. Others are human-made. The sky in Earth's **atmosphere** holds many interesting objects as well. We may not need a telescope to see them, but they are no less dazzling.

The **atmosphere** is the layer of gas that surrounds Earth.

# Stars

Stars are glowing balls of gases. They are grouped into galaxies. The Milky Way galaxy alone contains hundreds of billions of stars. Most stars are incredibly far away.

Nearly all stars are mostly made up of a gas called hydrogen. A star's core is very hot. Great pressure squeezes the core, causing some of the hydrogen to change into another gas, helium. This process makes the star shine.

**Stars are found in large groups called galaxies. Galaxies can contain billions of stars.**

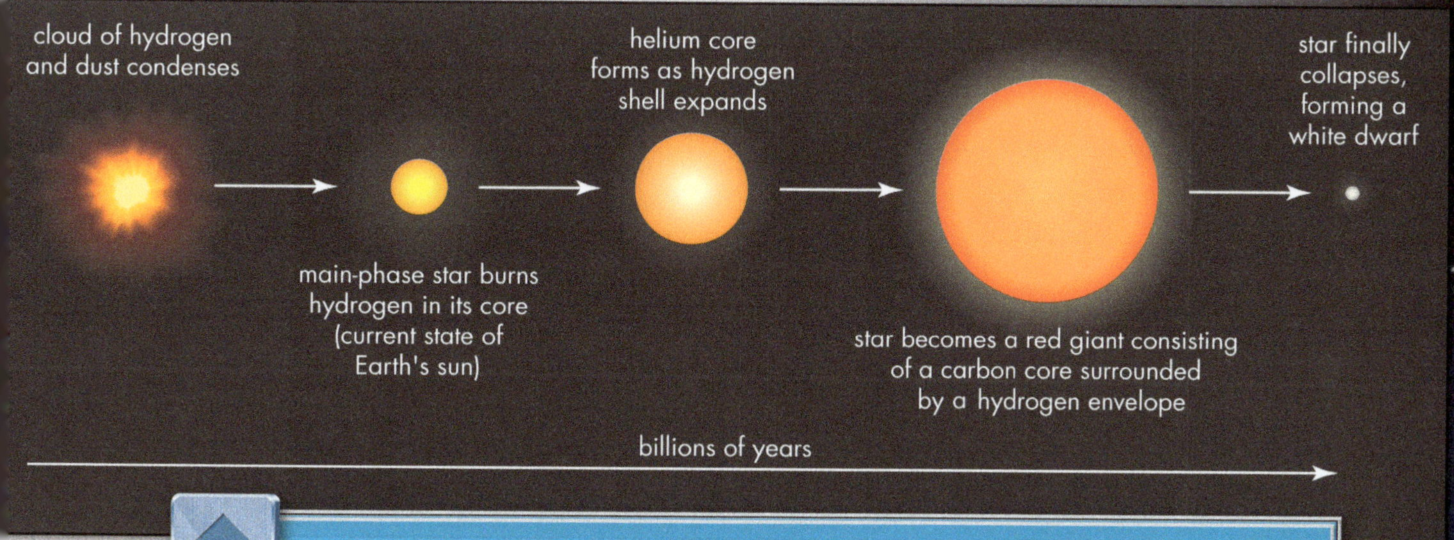


**A medium-sized star has a life span of billions of years.**

Stars may be different in size, temperature, brightness, and color. After shining for billions of years, a star uses up all of its hydrogen. Small and medium stars slowly cool down and stop shining. Large stars end with a violent explosion called a supernova.

### Think About It

The Sun is actually a star. Its size and brightness are average. What does this mean for the Sun's future?

# GALAXIES

A galaxy is a group of stars, clouds of gas, and dust particles that move together through the universe. There are billions of galaxies in the universe. They probably formed billions of years ago, soon after the universe began.

**Spiral galaxies** are shaped like pinwheels. Elliptical galaxies can look like a football. Irregular galaxies are unusually shaped.

The smaller galaxies are made up of millions of stars. The largest galaxies contain trillions of stars.

The Sun, Earth, and the other planets of the solar system are part of

The Whirlpool Galaxy is a **spiral galaxy** that can be seen easily through binoculars.

**The Andromeda Galaxy is the closest spiral galaxy to the Milky Way.**

the Milky Way galaxy. Most galaxies move through the universe as part of clusters, or groups, of galaxies. The Milky Way is at one end of a cluster called the Local Group. It includes more than 40 galaxies.

# LIGHTNING

Lightning is electricity released from Earth's atmosphere during thunderstorms. Water droplets inside a cloud carry positive and negative electrical charges. Lightning occurs when too many negative charges build up

The loud boom that follows lightning is called **thunder**. When electricity from lightning heats and expands gases in the air, they make a loud noise.

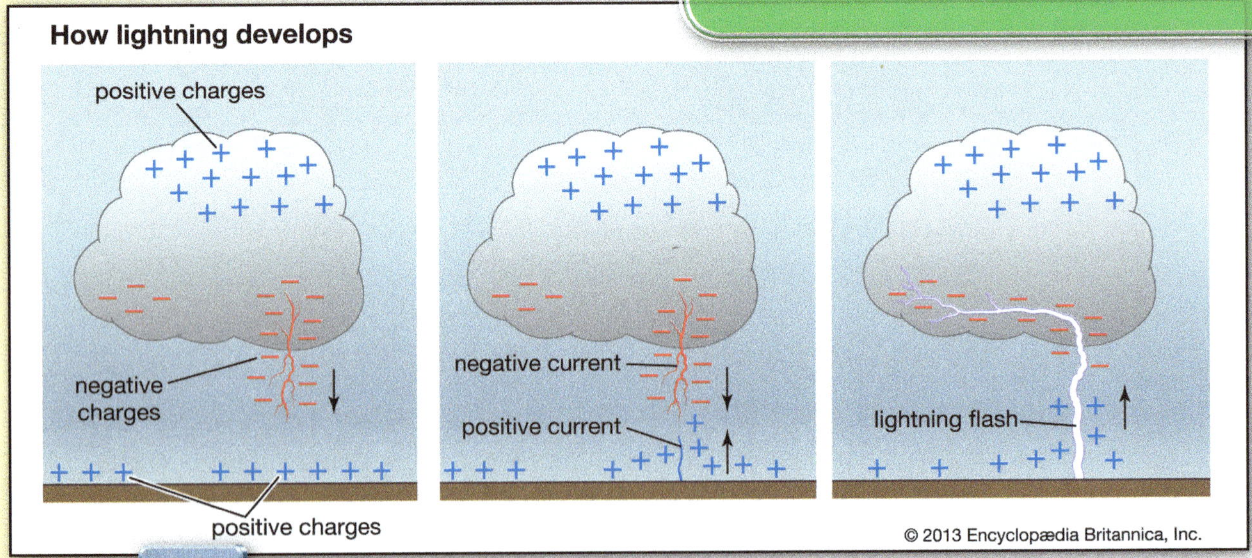


**This illustration shows how lightning forms in clouds.**

**Lightning looks dramatic when it flashes through a dark sky.**

in a cloud. To balance these negative charges, positive charges form on the ground. Because opposite charges attract, the negative charges in the cloud want to join the positive charges on the ground.

Eventually the cloud releases a strong, negatively charged electrical current. As the negative current heads toward the ground, a positively charged current jumps from the ground to meet it. When the currents join, they create a bright flash of lightning, followed by **thunder**.

# Meteoroids

A meteoroid is a chunk of rock or metal from space that falls through Earth's atmosphere. Most meteoroids burn up in the atmosphere. This creates a bright streak of light called a meteor. Meteors are also called shooting stars. If a meteoroid survives its fall and reaches Earth's surface, it is called a meteorite.

**This is the world's largest meteorite, known as the Hoba Meteorite.**

## Compare and Contrast

**Meteors, meteoroids, and meteorites all sound very similar. Compare and contrast the three objects.**

Almost all meteoroids are formed from material that breaks off of objects in space called comets or asteroids. The chunk of rock or metal may enter Earth's atmosphere traveling as fast as 45 miles (72 kilometers) per second. Most meteoroids melt from the heat or break up from the pressure within seconds of entering Earth's atmosphere.

The annual Geminid meteor shower can be seen from almost anywhere on Earth.

# Comets

A comet is a small chunk of ice and dust that orbits the Sun. It is sometimes described as a "dirty snowball."

Most comets travel very far into the solar system. It can take from several years to many thousands of years to complete one orbit. The best-known comet is Halley's Comet. It can be seen from Earth about every 76 years.

**Compare and Contrast**

**A comet's orbit is shaped like a long oval. Compare and contrast comet orbits to those of planets.**

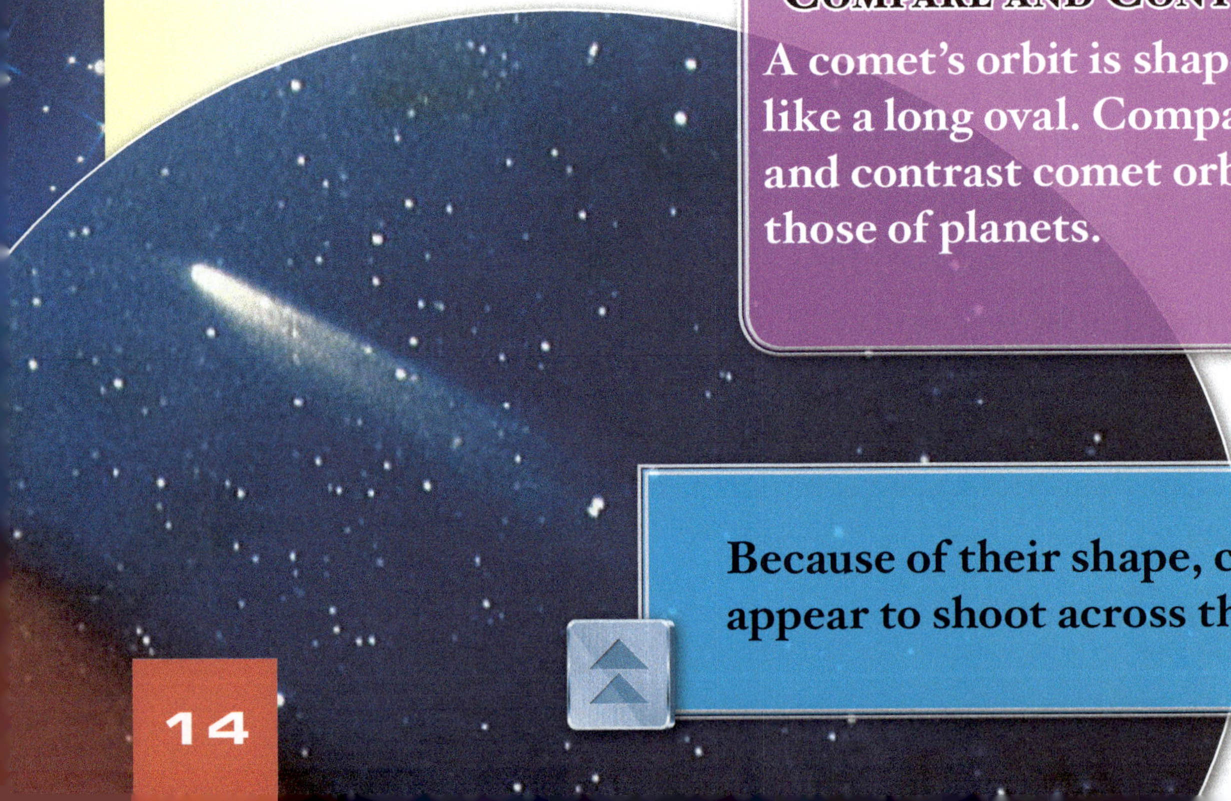

**Because of their shape, comets appear to shoot across the sky.**

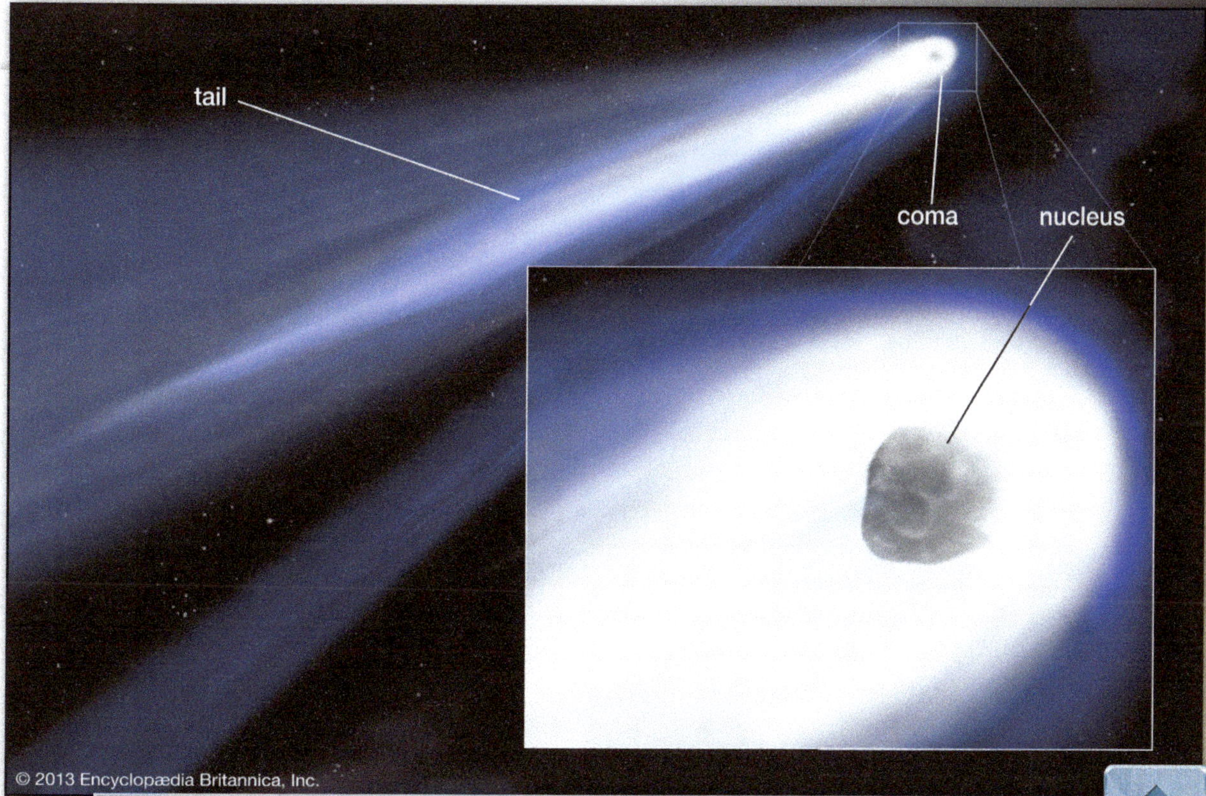


**A comet is made up of a nucleus, a coma, and a tail.**

The main part of a comet is called the nucleus. It is made of frozen water and gases plus dust and rock. When the comet gets close to the Sun, a cloud of gas and dust builds up around the comet. Eventually energy and particles from the Sun push some of the gas and dust out to form tails.

# Dwarf Planets

Dwarf planets are small planets. Like the eight planets of the solar system, they are large and round and orbit the Sun. The difference is that planets are large enough to affect the smaller bodies nearby. Planets are big enough to either push these bodies away or sweep them up. Dwarf planets are not big enough to do this.

Until recently, there was no classification of dwarf planets. In 2006, the International Astronomical Union decided that Pluto

**Once classified as a planet, Pluto is now considered a dwarf planet, or plutoid.**

**Compare and Contrast**

**Dwarf planets are smaller than the planet Mercury. Look up the diameters of dwarf planets and compare and contrast them to the other planets.**

was not a planet. Pluto had been considered the ninth planet of the solar system. Its category was changed to dwarf planet. Eris, Ceres, Makemake, and Haumea are other dwarf planets in our solar system.

**This artist's rendering shows the size of the dwarf planets Eris *(top)*, Ceres *(below Eris)*, and Pluto and its moon *(left)* compared to Earth and the Moon.**

# Artificial Satellites

A satellite is an object that orbits a larger object in space. Satellites can be natural or artificial (made by people). Artificial satellites are sent into space to gather information. Most are launched into space by rockets.

A **space station** is a special kind of satellite used by astronauts. Astronauts can live on a space station for months while they gather information and perform experiments.

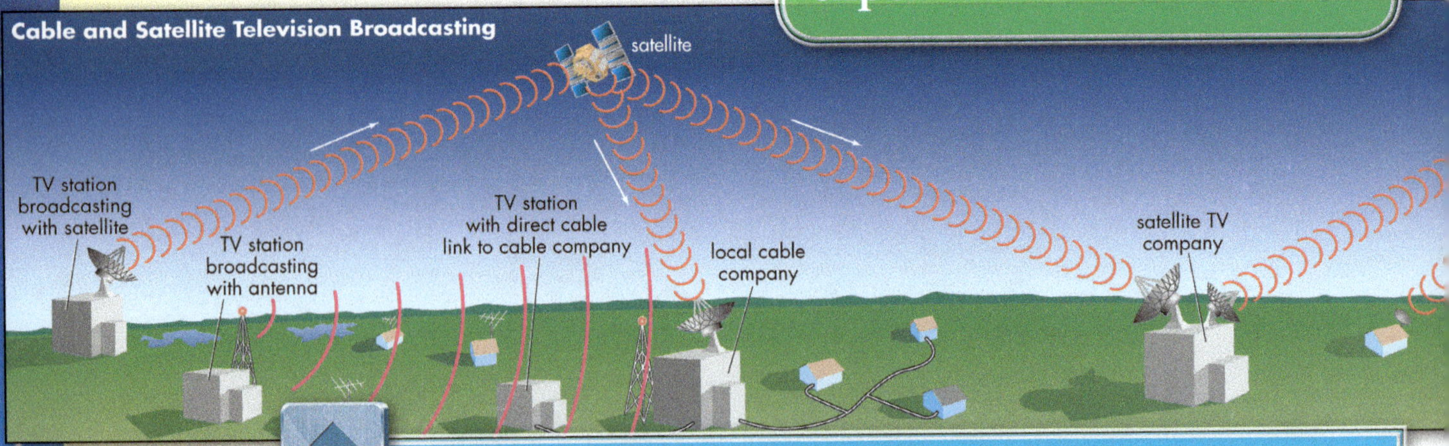


Artificial satellites can be used to broadcast television signals.

The International **Space Station** is an example of an artificial satellite.

Artificial satellites have many purposes. Scientific satellites collect information about space. The Hubble Space Telescope is a scientific satellite that orbits around Earth. It sees the sky more clearly than telescopes on the ground. Communications satellites help send telephone calls, radio and television programs, and computer information all over the world. Airplanes, ships, and cars with special equipment can use information from satellites to find their way from place to place. Military forces use satellites for spying. Satellites are also used in weather forecasting.

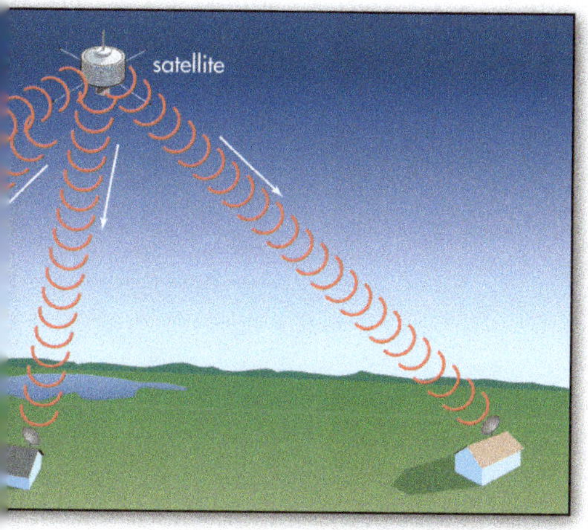

# Space Junk

Space is full of junk. Millions of pieces of debris orbit Earth. They travel at speeds up to 17,500 miles per hour (28,000 km/hour). These speeds are fast enough for debris to cause damage. Even a chip of paint from an abandoned space station could harm a spacecraft.

Space junk particles can be artificial or natural. Meteoroids are an example of natural debris. They orbit the Sun. Artificial debris can be anything that no longer works, such as old satellites or abandoned launches.

The U.S. military uses radar and telescopes to keep track

**This space debris sample was once part of a shuttle solid rocket booster.**

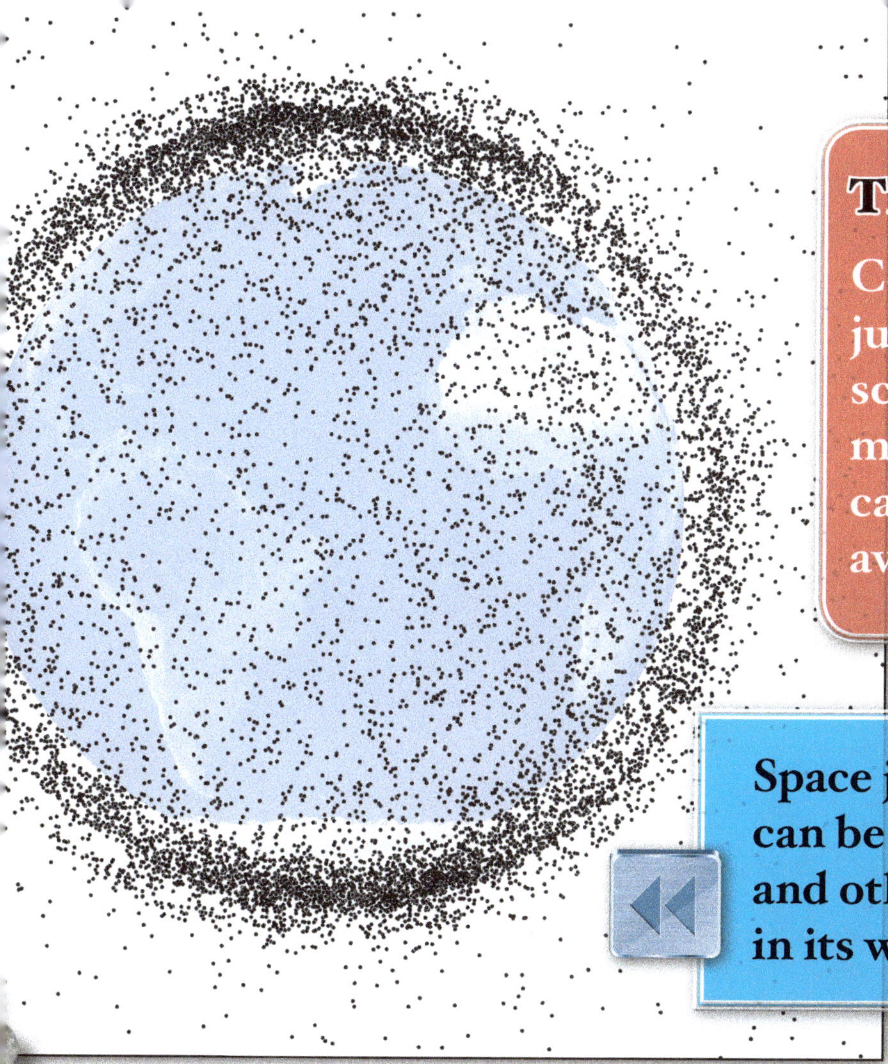

### Think About It

Collisions with space junk can cause the scattering of even more debris. How can such accidents be avoided?

**Space junk orbits Earth and can be a danger to satellites and other spacecraft that get in its way.**

of any space debris larger than a softball. If danger to astronauts is suspected, NASA plans a course of action for spacecraft to avoid the debris.

# Black Holes

A black hole is an area in space with an especially strong force called gravity. This gravity pulls in everything that gets close. Nothing, not even light, can escape from a black hole once it has been pulled in.

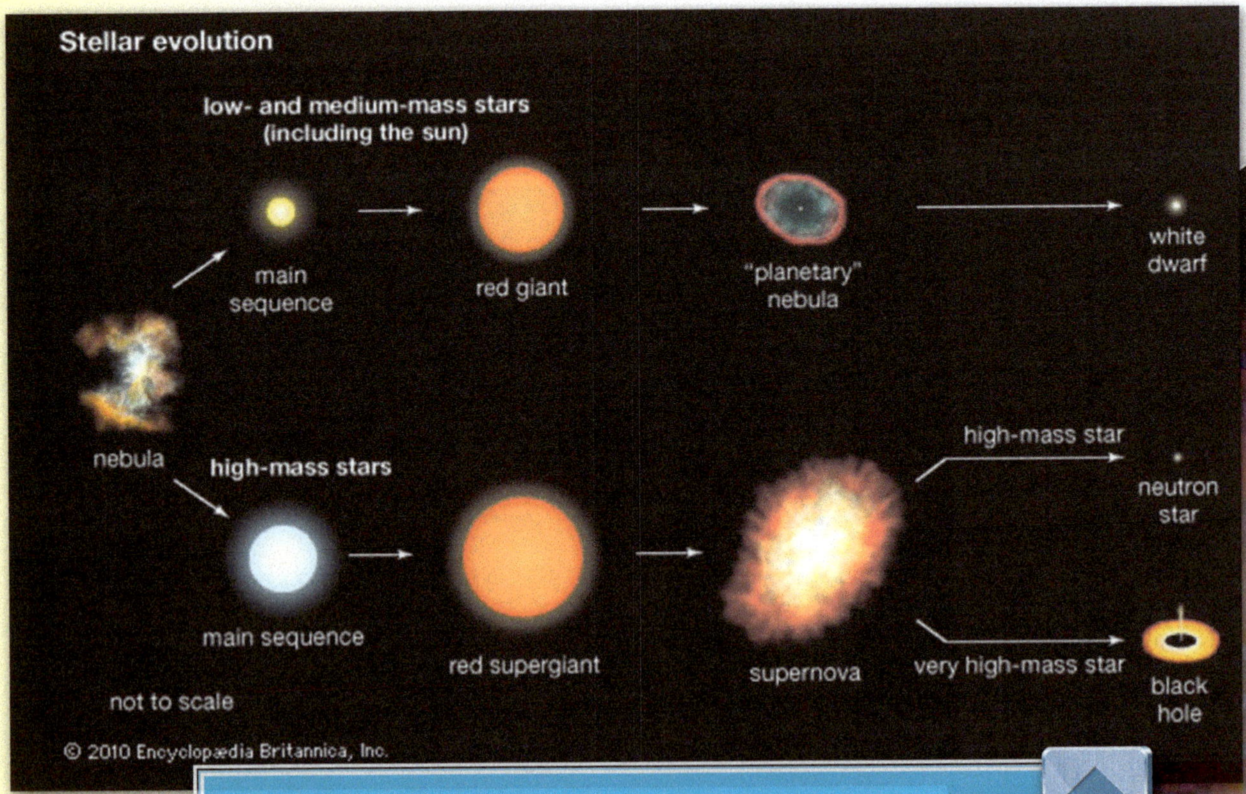


The evolution of a star depends on its mass. Stars with the highest masses become black holes.

**THINK ABOUT IT**

**Only stars that are more than three times as large as the Sun become black holes. Are black holes heavy or light?**

Black holes are not actually holes. They have great amounts of material packed in very tightly. They are called "black" because they are invisible.

A black hole can be formed when a huge star uses up its fuel. When a star runs out of its fuel, it cannot counter the gravity that pulls the star in on itself. The gravity crushes the star smaller and smaller, and it becomes a black hole.

**As gravity crushes high-mass stars, black holes are created.**

# AURORAS

Auroras are dazzling displays of colored light that sometimes appear in the night sky. They occur in Earth's far northern and far southern regions. In the Northern Hemisphere such a display is known as

**The northern lights are seen here in late winter above Manitoba, Canada.**

This spectacular display of the aurora borealis lights up the sky in Iceland.

**Compare and Contrast**

Auroras are caused by the Sun. Compare and contrast auroras with lightning, which is electricity released during thunderstorms.

aurora borealis, or the northern lights. In the Southern Hemisphere it is called aurora australis, or the southern lights. Auroras are named after Aurora, the ancient Roman goddess of the dawn.

Auroras take many shapes and forms, with arcs and rays of colored light being the most common. The light may look like shimmering curtains, bands, waves, or clouds. An aurora constantly changes shape as the light moves across the sky. The light may also alternately brighten and fade.

# Rainbows

A rainbow is a multicolored arc, or curved line, in the sky. Rainbows form when the Sun's rays strike raindrops falling from faraway clouds. Rainbows appear in the part of the sky opposite the Sun, usually in the early morning or late afternoon. From inside to outside, the colors of a rainbow are violet, indigo, blue, green, yellow, orange, and red.

Sunlight travels through space in the form of waves. Light waves with different wavelengths appear as

A **primary bow** emerges over a beach in Hawaii.

different colors. Usually all light waves blend together to form white light. But when light waves pass through raindrops, they separate. The separated light waves appear as the colors of a rainbow.

**Light reflected through a prism has the same effect as a rainbow. The prism separates the ray into seven colors.**

A **primary bow** is the brightest and most common type of rainbow. A double rainbow is called a secondary bow.

# Explaining Objects in the Sky

People no longer believe ancient stories and myths that explain the stars in the sky and other happenings. Thanks to advances in astronomy—the study of all objects outside Earth's atmosphere—we know why the Sun appears to rise each morning. We understand where lightning comes from.

Strong cameras and telescopes allow astronomers to observe distant objects. The Hubble Space Telescope orbits

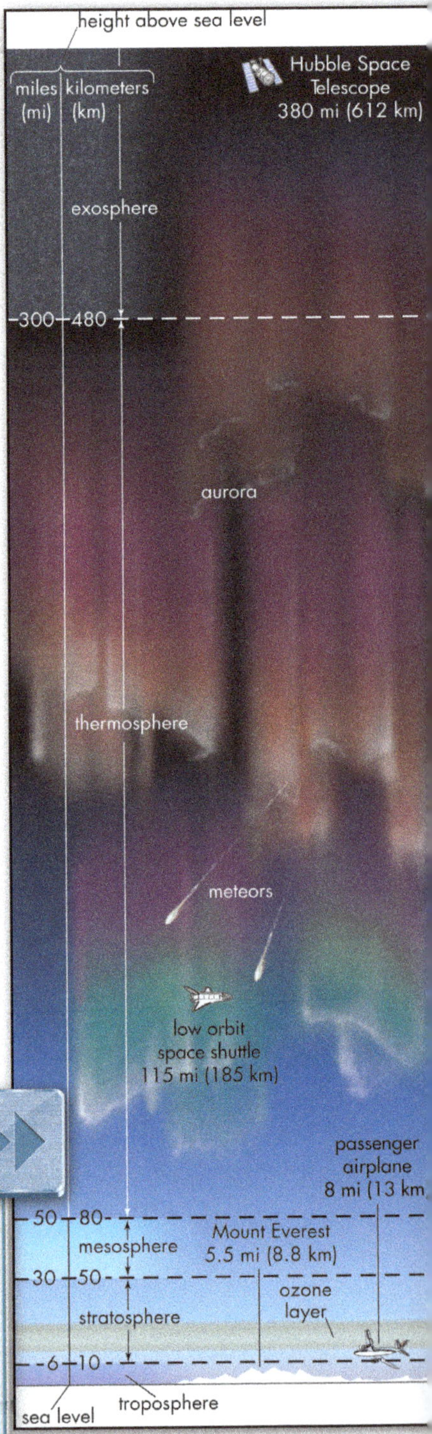


**The Hubble Space Telescope can view space more clearly than telescopes on Earth can because it orbits above Earth's atmosphere.**

## Think About It

**Before calendars and clocks, people looked to the Sun and the stars. How do you think they used objects in the sky to keep track of time?**

around Earth as a floating observatory. It magnifies and records images of distant space objects. It then sends the information to astronomers on Earth. Other spacecraft also have gathered information about the Sun, Moon, and planets. For as much as we know, however, space still contains mysteries.

**The Hubble Space Telescope has allowed astronomers to learn much more about space.**

# Glossary

**artificial** Not natural; made by humans.
**asteroids** Rocky bodies between Mars and Jupiter, with diameters from a fraction of a mile to nearly 500 miles (805 km).
**astronomers** Scientists who study space.
**auroras** Dazzling displays of colored light that sometimes appear in the night sky.
**black hole** An area in space where gravity pulls in everything that gets close.
**comets** Bright heavenly bodies that develop a cloudy tail as they move closer to the Sun in their orbits.
**constellations** Groups of stars that form a pattern.
**debris** The remains of something broken or destroyed.
**dwarf planet** Body that orbits the Sun but that is smaller than other planets.
**galaxies** Any of the very large groups of stars and other matter that are found throughout the universe.
**gravity** The natural force of attraction between particles or bodies that occurs because of their mass.
**meteor** A piece of rock or metal that burns brightly as it falls into Earth's atmosphere.
**meteorite** A meteor that reaches the surface of Earth.
**meteoroid** A meteor revolving around the Sun.
**Milky Way** The galaxy that contains Earth, the Sun, and the Moon.
**observatory** A place from which scientists study the sky.
**orbit** The path taken by one body circling around another body.
**satellite** A natural body or human-made object that orbits Earth, the Moon, or another heavenly body.
**stars** Balls of gas of enormous mass that produce their own light.
**supernova** The explosion of a very large star.
**telescope** An instrument used to see objects in outer space.

# For More Information

## Books

Graham, Ian. *Comets and Asteroids* (Discovering Space). Mankato, MN: Smart Apple Media, 2008.

Kortenkamp, Steve. *Asteroids, Comets, and Meteoroids* (Fact Finders). Mankato, MN: Capstone Press, 2012.

Miller, Ron. *Satellites* (Space Innovations). Minneapolis, MN: Twenty-First Century Books, 2008.

Trammel, Howard K. *The Solar System* (True Books: Space). New York, NY: Children's Press, 2009.

Waxman, Laura Hamilton. *Exploring Black Holes* (Searchlight Books). Minneapolis, MN: Lerner Publications, 2012.

Waxman, Laura Hamilton. *Exploring the International Space Station* (Searchlight Books). Minneapolis, MN: Lerner Publications, 2012.

## Websites

Because of the changing nature of Internet links, Rosen Publishing has developed an online list of websites related to the subject of this book. This site is updated regularly. Please use this link to access the list:

http://www.rosenlinks.com/lfo/sky

# Index